Defending Orcas

NO MORE CAPTIVITY

Captain Paul Watson
Tiffany Humphrey

GroundSwell Books
SUMMERTOWN, TENNESSEE

Library of Congress Cataloging-in-Publication Data available upon request.

GROUNDSWELL BOOKS

SOLUTIONS FOR A SUSTAINABLE WORLD

We chose to print this title on paper certified by The Forest Steward-
ship Council® (FSC®), a global, not-for-profit organization dedicated
to the promotion of responsible forest management worldwide.

MIX
Paper from
responsible sources
FSC® C001701

Stock photography: 123 RF
Cover and interior design: John Wincek

Printed in Hong Kong

GroundSwell Books
an imprint of Book Publishing Company
PO Box 99
Summertown, TN 38483
888-260-8458
bookpubco.com

ISBN: 978-1-939053-36-7

27 26 25 24 23 22   1 2 3 4 5 6 7 8 9

CONTENTS

1

All about Orcas

Orcas are some of the most magnificent creatures in the ocean. They are part of the same group, or order, of sea mammals as whales, called Cetaceans. Orcas are sometimes called "killer whales" because of how they may work together to hunt whales. But orcas aren't really whales—they're actually the largest member of the dolphin family.

Orca Facts

Orcas grow to be about 30 feet (9 m) in length, and in the wild they often live for thirty to fifty years—sometimes even longer. Their typical black-and-white markings not only make them easy for us to recognize but also give the orcas some camouflage when underwater. Be sure to notice the patches of gray, known as saddles, behind their dorsal fins. These saddles are distinctive markings that vary from orca to orca.

It's estimated that there are fifty thousand orcas around the world. Although orcas can be found in many different regions and climates, they are most prevalent in the colder waters of the ocean. Groups of

around twenty orcas, known as pods, often consist of generations of family members that stay together and develop their own unique forms of communication. The oldest female in a pod will be the leader. Although orcas enjoy eating a wide variety of sea creatures (such as seals, sharks, and fish), individual pods will sometimes develop a taste for one type of fish or sea mammal over another.

Orcas have developed a distinct language through a process known as echolocation. They'll send out a call and then listen for how that call echoes off objects in their environment in order to identify and locate those objects. Orcas also create specific types of calls that help them identify family members and pod mates as well as communicate about dangers and available prey.

Orcas have developed an interesting strategy for sleeping while they're in the water. Instead of drifting off and losing consciousness, as humans do, an orca will simply turn off half of its brain at a time! Orcas can't breathe automatically like we do when we sleep; an orca breathes only when it needs to. Keeping half of its brain alert allows it to take a breath while the other half of its brain rests. Orcas will alternate which half of their brain goes to sleep, giving each part of the brain a chance to rejuvenate.

KINGDOM	PHYLUM	CLASS	ORDER	INFRAORDER	FAMILY	GENUS	SPECIES
Animalia	Chordata	Mammalia	Artiodactyla	Cetacea	Delphinidae	Orcinus	Orca

melon (echolocation) • blowhole • dorsal fin • saddle patch • teeth • eye • ear • flipper • flukes

Types of Orcas

In the North Pacific Ocean, where orcas are most widely studied, three types of orcas have been identified. Resident orcas in that part of the world are found from Russia to California and prefer to eat fish. Scientists classify resident orcas into smaller groups, the most well known being the southern resident orcas (found from San Francisco to southeastern Alaska) and northern resident orcas (found from southern British Columbia to southeastern Alaska). There is also a group in southern Alaska and another in western Alaska and the northern Pacific.

Transient orcas live in smaller groups along the coast of the Pacific Northwest. Their dorsal fins tend to stand straighter than those of resident orcas. Transient orcas like to hunt in groups and will feed on a wider variety of animals than resident orcas. Offshore orcas, which live miles from land, are smaller and have rounder dorsal fins.

The Challenges Orcas Face

Orcas are experiencing increased threats to their environment. They can become entangled in fishing nets, sickened from chemicals dumped into the ocean, and disoriented from the noise of passing ships and the detonation of explosives. The depletion of fish and the other animals orcas feed on forces orca pods to travel farther for food and compete with other orcas and other species for what's available.

COMMERCIAL FISHING
Purse seine

Several specific events have had fateful impacts on certain groups of orcas. In 1989, the oil tanker *Exxon Valdez* spilled as much as 11 million gallons of crude oil into the ocean waters off Alaska, killing off one group of transient orcas in the Pacific Northwest. Finally, the capture of orcas for display at marine parks has caused a serious reduction in other orca populations, especially the southern resident orcas of the North Pacific Ocean. Only half as many orcas in that group are alive today as there were a century ago, and they are struggling to maintain this number.

Scientists continue to monitor orcas so we can understand more about their unique abilities and how they can be protected from hazards caused by humans. Satellite tracking tags placed on certain orcas can be followed to show where they migrate during the winter, what they eat, and exactly how far they travel. Digital recording tags allow researchers to learn more about the sounds orcas send and receive and how they're affected by man-made noise. Blood samples taken from orca mothers and babies show whether contaminants are being passed when babies nurse. Photography and monitoring devices help scientists measure the number of orcas in different populations so they can determine whether conservation work is helping these populations increase.

Does Government Protection Work?

The International Whaling Commission (IWC) was formed in 1946 by fifteen whaling nations to protect and manage the number of whales available for commercial fishing. There are now eighty-eight nations that are part of the IWC. In 1982, the commission voted to ban commercial whaling entirely except for scientific research. Its current mission is to safeguard whales and other marine mammals and allow the whale population to grow back to what it was before commercial whaling began.

The IWC also funds efforts to conserve orcas, dolphins, and other cetaceans. However, even with these regulations, orcas that were thought to be a nuisance because they stole fish from fishing boats were routinely shot and killed in great numbers. Japanese whalers slaughtered almost 1,200 orcas between 1954 and 1997, and Norwegian whalers killed about 2,400 orcas between 1938 and 1980.

The governments of both the United States and Canada have passed laws to protect orcas from human activities and improve their chances for survival. In 1972, the US Congress passed the Marine Mammal Protection Act. Its mission was to prevent the number of marine mammals, such as orcas and whales, from becoming so few that there wouldn't be enough of them to maintain balance in their environments. (Ideally, these mammals will feed on smaller animals and fish, keeping those populations at a stable number, and then their decomposing bodies will feed other organisms in the environment.) However, the Marine Mammal Protection Act does not stop people from taking marine mammals for public display or prohibit the commercial fishing of orcas for scientific research.

In 1973, the US Congress passed the Endangered Species Act (ESA) to protect endangered species and their ecosystems (the environments in which they live). Under the ESA, southern resident orcas are listed as endangered. Their population declined drastically about fifty years ago due to being hunted and being captured for display at marine parks. Researchers believe their numbers are still low, because commercial fishing has severely depleted the quantity of salmon the southern resident orcas like to eat.

Which agencies protect which species in the United States:

- Animal and Plant Health Inspection Service of the Department of Agriculture protects captive marine mammals.
- National Marine Fisheries Service of the Department of Commerce protects dolphins, porpoises, sea lions, seals, and whales.
- US Fish and Wildlife Service of the Department of the Interior protects otters, polar bears, manatees, and walrus.

In 2016, Canada launched the Oceans Protection Plan, a wide-ranging program to increase marine safety and save ecosystems. Then it enacted the Whales Initiative in 2018 specifically to support several marine mammal populations, one of them being the southern resident orcas. Other countries have also adopted their own agreements. New Zealand enacted a Marine Mammals Protection Act in 1978, and Australia adopted the Whale Protection Act in 1980.

Unfortunately, not all the member countries of the IWC are following the whaling ban, and whale hunting continues. Certain businesses within the United States and Canada, as well as foreign nations, continue to defy the work done by environmentalists to protect orcas and other marine mammals.

A limited number of animals are allowed to be killed for scientific research or by Native or First Nations peoples who rely on these animals for food. But commercial interests claiming to be doing research or providing food for Indigenous communities try to push the boundaries of these exceptions in the protection laws. Sea Shepherd continues to confront the illegal actions of countries or businesses that disregard whaling bans.

2

The Hunting and Capturing of Orcas

Since the mid-1800s, marine mammals have been caught and imprisoned for entertainment. The famous circus owner P. T. Barnum displayed dolphins and beluga whales as part of his circus acts. In the late 1800s, aquariums in England displayed harbor porpoises. By the 1870s, whales and dolphins were being captured and sold to parks in the United States and Europe, which led to the injury and death of many of these beautiful sea animals.

Orcas as Marine Park Attractions

Marine parks were opened as a way for businesspeople to make money training orcas and dolphins to perform. Marineland (first known as Marine Studios) opened in Florida in 1938 and housed bottlenose dolphins. Marineland of the Pacific opened in the Los Angeles area in 1954; it was eventually taken over by SeaWorld and its marine animals were moved to San Diego. Miami Seaquarium opened its doors in 1955 and to this day continues to house just one orca, a lone female named Lolita.

The act of capturing orcas for study and display has had very sad consequences for the orcas themselves. The region around the San Juan Islands, in the coastal waters between Seattle and Vancouver, is home to several large groups of orcas. It's estimated that more than one hundred orcas lived there in the early 1970s. But because so many of them were captured for display at sea parks around the world, the population had dropped to almost half that number by 1976.

The first orca was captured off the coast of Washington State in 1961 and taken to Marineland of the Pacific, where she died two days later from severe distress. The next year, wildlife hunters for Marineland went back to capture more orcas and pursued a male and female that were traveling together. The female was lassoed by the Marineland crew, and she called out to her mate for help. When both orcas charged the boat, they were shot. The male disappeared, but the female, now dead, was taken back to shore and processed for dog food.

In 1964, the Vancouver Aquarium commissioned an artist to kill an orca in order to make a life-size sculpture for an aquarium exhibit. He harpooned a young orca about six years old, and while it struggled to survive, members of its pod came to the young animal's aid, pushing it to the surface to breathe. Even though it was then shot several times, it managed to survive this assault. The manager of the Vancouver Aquarium decided to have the young orca towed for over sixteen hours back to Vancouver and placed in a sea pen, where it could be seen by visitors to the aquarium. This is the first record we have of an orca being on public display. Sadly, this orca died three months later.

In 1970, eighty orcas were caught in a net in the San Juan Islands. From this group, seven were selected to be sent to marine parks. Only one orca from that capture remains alive in captivity today, and that is Lolita in Miami, Florida.

The Story of Namu and Shamu

In the 1960s, word started getting out that fishermen could make a profit selling orcas, so they captured the orcas that ended up in their fishing nets instead of releasing them. In 1965, a captured orca was sold to the Seattle Public Aquarium, where he was named Namu.

The staff at the aquarium tried to capture a female orca to mate with Namu. They ended up harpooning a mother orca with a baby. The mother drowned while she was being towed back to Seattle, but her female calf survived the trip. The young orca was promptly named Shamu, a combination of *she* and *Namu*, and she was the first of several female orcas to be given that name.

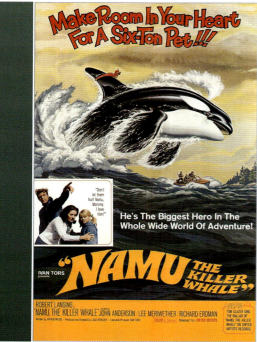

A movie was made about Namu called *Namu, the Killer Whale*. It was a fictitious story about two people who became friends with an orca and tried to save it from threats from fishermen. Right before the movie was released, the real-life Namu died from an infection caused by polluted water in his sea pen.

A terrible incident happened to Shamu years later, after she was shipped to SeaWorld San Diego. A woman who worked for SeaWorld was asked to get into Shamu's pool so she could pose for pictures with the orca to promote the Shamu exhibit. After climbing onto the orca's back, she rode Shamu around the pool one time, and then Shamu began to buck. After the woman was thrown into the water, Shamu grabbed hold of her leg and pushed her around the pool, periodically dunking her just under the water's surface. The woman was rescued, but this was eventually seen as a foolish act that put her in great danger. From that time forward, trainers were not allowed back in the water with Shamu. Sadly, just four months later, Shamu died from an infection.

TILIKUM

Tilikum was captured off Iceland in 1983 at the age of two. He first was sent to Sealand of the Pacific (a public aquarium in British Columbia, Canada), where he was kept at night with two other orcas in a pool measuring only 25 feet by 30 feet (7.5 m by 9 m). He later was moved to SeaWorld Orlando. At both places, he was involved in the injury and death of several trainers. After thirty-three years in captivity, Tilikum died of a bad lung infection.

The Soviet Union killed 916 orcas in the waters off Antarctica between 1979 and 1980. Prior to this massive slaughter, the Soviets typically took approximately 25 orcas per whaling season.

Orca Hunting in the Caribbean

As recently as 2018, orcas have been hunted for their meat near a small island nation in the eastern Caribbean called Saint Vincent and the Grenadines. The nation is exempt from the global moratorium on whaling that was issued in 1982 by the IWC. Between 2000 and 2015, Saint Vincent islanders slaughtered twenty-eight humpback whales, which have been endangered since 1970.

Even though the IWC funds work to conserve smaller ocean mammals, such as orcas, it does not regulate the killing of them. Fishermen from Saint Vincent have hunted hundreds of dolphins, orcas, pilot whales, and porpoises every year since the early 1900s. There is a small market for their meat on the nearby island of Barbados, even though orcas are known to contain high levels of lead, mercury, and polychlorinated biphenyls (PCBs), which are dangerous chemicals found in plastics. (Although PCBs are banned today, they continue to be found in some of the foods we eat.)

In 2017, Saint Vincent opened a new airport in order to boost tourism and promote itself as a destination spot for whale watching, scuba diving, and other water sports. Sadly, that same year, passengers on a touring boat were watching a pod of four orcas when a hunting boat approached and killed two of the orcas with a harpoon gun. Although the island government has talked about banning the hunting of orcas, there has been no ban put into place. Sea Shepherd Conservation Society is currently working with local officials to end this barbaric practice.

3

CHAPTER

The Problems of Orcas in Captivity

Life is very difficult, even deadly, for any wild animal in confinement, and this is true for orcas as well. Marine parks attempt to provide adequate food and health care as well as activities to prevent boredom. However, a concrete tank is a poor substitute for the open ocean that is the natural habitat for orcas.

Emotional Stress

Confinement causes emotional problems for orcas, and they'll act out in a number of ways to reduce their stress. Sometimes they'll fight boredom simply by regurgitating some of the fish they eat so they can play with the birds that swoop down to investigate what's floating on the surface of the orca tanks. But often their stressful behaviors are self-destructive. Some orcas will attack the walls of their tanks, gnawing on them and ramming their heads into them. They'll also bite the metal railings between tanks. At times this behavior is so harsh that the orcas will die from self-inflicted wounds.

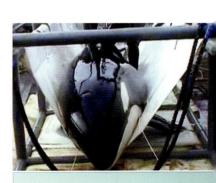

The same auditory signals (known as echolocation) that allow orcas in the wild to identify the objects in the ocean turn their smooth-surfaced tanks into a disorienting echo chamber. Sea Shepherd created the Tilikum Tank, a portable enclosure to let people experience for themselves what captivity is like for these animals. The floor and walls are covered with mirrors to duplicate the orcas' tiny underwater prisons, which constantly throw back their own reflections and echoed voices. (In addition, the orcas have to deal with the sound of show music blasting at full volume from the marine park.) The public is invited to spend a few minutes in this tank of mirrors, but many people find it difficult to stay inside the Tilikum Tank for even that short amount of time.

Even if orcas are kept in large tanks, they often have to share their space with orcas that came from completely different parts of the world. These animals would never come in contact with each other in the wild. They speak different dialects and have different diets as well. Imagine being in an enclosed space with people who don't speak your language and are competing with you for food and the attention of your captors!

CALYPSO AND CLOVIS

Calypso and Clovis were kept in the same tank in Marineland of Antibes, France, but they came from very different parts of the world. Calypso was a northern resident female from British Columbia, and Clovis was a southern resident male from off the coast of Washington State. They had different dialects and would not have interacted in the wild. After Calypso died, Clovis lived another two and a half years alone.

Stress behavior also results from removing orcas from the stable order of their pods when they're captured or when they are shuttled among various marine parks. Parents and children will show signs of stress if they are separated. Larger, older orcas will often physically intimidate younger orcas, sometimes scratching them with their teeth, a behavior known as raking.

KETO

Keto is a male orca that currently resides at Loro Parque in the Canary Islands. After being separated from his mother, he became aggressive toward his trainers. One day, while performing tricks, he missed a few cues and was denied some fish treats as a result. Frustrated, he lashed out at his trainer, dragging him to the bottom of the pool until the man drowned.

Training orcas to perform tricks on command is a very unnatural and stressful activity for the animals. Trainers will ride on the orcas' backs or get them to leap in the air. This can frustrate some orcas to the breaking point. Eventually, they may turn on their trainers, either injuring them or, as has happened in a few cases, drowning them. Marine parks have tried to document aggression by orcas toward trainers in order to understand the signals the orcas might give that they're about to attack, such as lunging at a trainer or mouthing a trainer's foot or leg. But not all orcas will show these signs beforehand.

Physical Stress

Besides emotional stress, orcas can suffer from a number of physical problems during confinement in tanks. The most common cause of death for captive dolphins and orcas is bacterial pneumonia, an infection of the lungs. Captivity causes stress to an orca's immune system, leaving it susceptible to these types of infections. Consequently, orcas are fed large quantities of antibiotics on a daily basis to fight these frequent infections; but when antibiotics are given too often, they can lose their effectiveness. That can leave the orcas with a dangerous resistance to the drugs while leaving the staff incapable of treating the orcas for further infections, such as those from cuts or bites.

Many of the orcas in captivity bite on the concrete sides of their tanks and the steel gates that separate them. This can fracture their teeth, exposing the soft interior, or pulp, of the teeth, and often leads to infections. Infected teeth are drilled (without the use of pain medication), so they can be rinsed with a solution of salt and iodine. This treatment is not always effective, and orcas have died when dental infections spread to other parts of their bodies.

LUNA AND MIRACLE

Luna was a southern resident male that became separated from his pod near Vancouver Island, British Columbia, and remained in the area for almost five years. He was particularly curious about any small boats that came near him. Despite efforts to reunite him with his pod, he was pulled into a tugboat propeller and killed. Miracle was a southern resident female orca that also had propeller wounds when she arrived at Sealand of the Pacific. She died five years later under mysterious circumstances.

Orcas in captivity spend far more time floating at the surface than than they do in the wild, and trainers have reported large swarms of mosquitoes on their backsides. Several orcas have either tested positive for or died of West Nile virus, which is spread through the bites of infected mosquitos. There has not been a single case of this virus found in wild

orcas. Another problem that only affects orcas in captivity is sun damage. Again, because they spend much more time on the surface of the water in their tanks than they would in the wild, their eyes can become sun damaged and their skin sunburned.

The diet of thawed frozen fish commonly fed to orcas in captivity can cause dehydration because thawed frozen food doesn't contain as much moisture as fresh food. Therefore, orcas must be fed quantities of tasteless gelatin cubes to match the water content they would normally get from their natural diet of fresh fish.

All of the adult male orcas in captivity (as well as some females) have collapsed dorsal fins. This condition rarely occurs in the wild and is usually associated with human interaction (such as when orcas get entangled in fishing lines). Dorsal fins might collapse because of the amount of time captive orcas spend on the surface, where their dorsal fins are above water and not getting any support. The collapse of dorsal fins can also be caused by dehydration and stress.

Keeping Track of Orca Deaths

The number of orcas that have died in captivity is very troubling. Marine parks have become more reluctant to publish information on the causes of death of these magnificent animals because they don't want any bad publicity that would result. At this time, SeaWorld reports orca deaths only to the National Marine Fisheries Service, the federal agency responsible for monitoring fish populations in US waters.

SeaWorld was eventually required to publicly release descriptions of the orcas they had in captivity. These descriptions include information on each orca's condition. In the pages that follow, we will introduce you to some of these orcas so you'll have a better idea of who they are and where they are located.

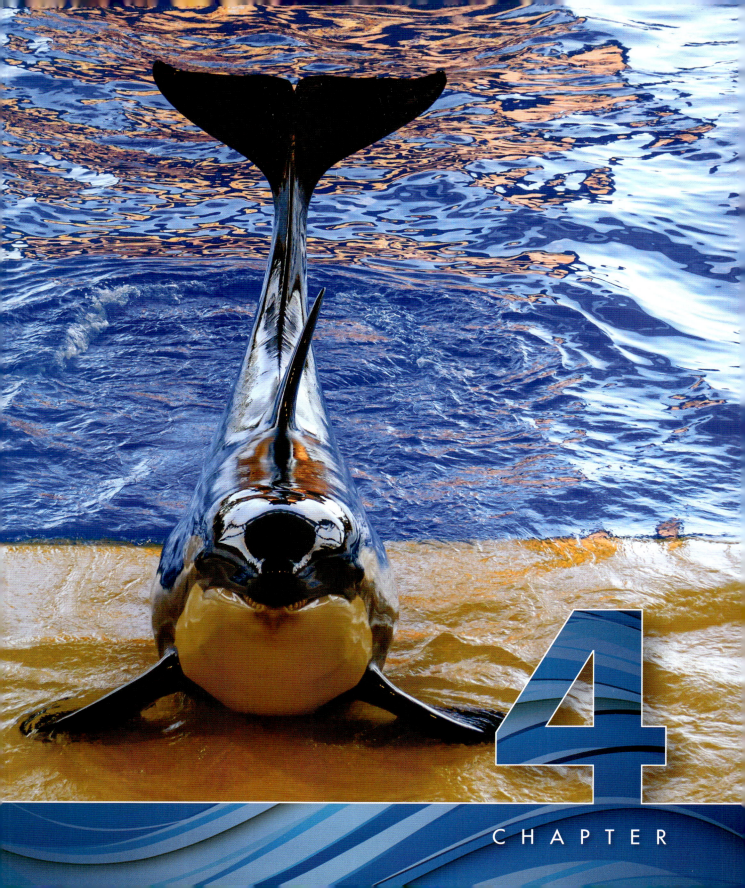

CHAPTER 4

Orcas in Marine Parks

Orcas can weigh from 5,000 to 12,000 pounds each—that's as much as one or two SUVs. These are heavy, muscular carnivores that are capable of causing death with a single blow. This makes it important to keep track of captive orca behavior. Warning signs have been recorded so trainers can anticipate when an act of aggression might occur. Unfortunately, not all animals give early warnings of trouble, and four humans have been killed in marine parks.

On the following pages, there are brief descriptions of many of the orcas in captivity. While not every incident of aggression has been recorded, the descriptions point to some of the frustrations that the animals in marine parks endure. Shockingly, no humans have ever been killed by orcas in the wild. Even during the violent whale captures off the coast of the Pacific Northwest, there have been no injuries inflicted on any people by the whales. Even as babies were ripped away from mothers, the whales still caused no injuries or death, not to one single person.

SEAWORLD SAN DIEGO, USA

SEAWORLD SAN ANTONIO, USA

SEAWORLD ORLANDO, USA

MIAMI SEAQUARIUM, USA

Marineland
Antibes, France
Inouk, Keijo, Moana, Wikie
4

Marineland
Niagara Falls, Ontario, Canada
Kiska
1

SeaWorld
San Diego, California, USA
Amaya, Corky II, Ikaika, Kalia, Keet, Makani, Nakai, Orkid, Shouka, Ulises
10

Miami Seaquarium
Miami, Florida, USA
Lolita
1

SeaWorld
San Antonio, Texas, USA
Kamea, Kyuquot, Sakari, Takara, Tuar
5

SeaWorld
Orlando, Florida, USA
Katina, Makaio, Malia, Nalani, Trua
5

Loro Parque
Canary Islands, Spain
Adàn, Keto, Kohana, Morgan, Skyla, Tekoa, Ula
7

Mundo Marino
San Clemente del Tuyú, Argentina
Kshamenk
1

MARINELAND, CANADA

MARINELAND, ANTIBES, FRANCE

LORO PARQUE, SPAIN

MUNDO MARINO, ARGENTINA

MOSKVARIUM, RUSSIA

PORT OF NAGOYA, JAPAN

KAMOGAWA SEA WORLD, JAPAN

Moskvarium
Moscow, Russia
Naja, Narnia, Nord
3

Seaside Dolphinarium
Nakhodka, Russia
Malvina
1

Kamogawa Sea World
Chiba, Japan
Lara, Lovey, Luna, Ran II
4

Port of Nagoya
Nagoya, Japan
Earth, Stella, Rin
3

Chimelong Ocean Kingdom
Hengqin, Zhuhai, China
Grace, Nukka, Orpheus, Tyson, 5 Unnamed
9

Shanghai Haichang Ocean Park
Shanghai, China
Dora, Wow, 2 Unnamed
4

Wuxi Changqiao Ocean Kingdom
Wuxi, China
2 Unnamed
2

CHIMELONG OCEAN KINGDOM, CHINA

WUXI CHANGQIAO OCEAN KINGDOM, CHINA

SHANGHAI HAICHANG OCEAN PARK, CHINA

Kamea

Makaio

Kayla and Malia

Nalani

Trua

Lolita

United States

SEAWORLD ORLANDO

SeaWorld Orlando was founded in 1973 and has held orcas captive since 1975.

Katina. Born around 1975 and captured at age three, Katina was the first mother to successfully give birth in captivity. She currently is the dominant female at SeaWorld Orlando.

Makaio. Born at SeaWorld Orlando in 2010.

Malia. Born at SeaWorld Orlando in 2007, Malia has shown several abnormal behaviors ranging from immobility to seizure-like states.

Nalani. Nalani was born at SeaWorld Orlando in 2006. For the first two months of her life, her mother, Katina, would often push her away. Fortunately, Nalani was still able to nurse and develop.

Trua. Born at SeaWorld Orlando in 2005, Trua spent months focused on the caulking in one of the pools, resulting in Sea-World having to remove the entire caulking in that pool.

MIAMI SEAQUARIUM

The Miami Seaquarium was founded in 1955 and has held orcas captive since 1968.

Lolita. Born around 1966 and captured at age four, Lolita is one of the oldest orcas in captivity. In 2015, she was included on the endangered list of the southern resident orca distinct population segment.

SEAWORLD SAN ANTONIO

SeaWorld San Antonio was founded in 1988 and has held orcas captive since that time.

Kamea. Kamea was born at SeaWorld San Antonio in 2013.

Kyuquot. Kyuquot was born at Sealand of the Pacific in 1991 and sent to SeaWorld San Antonio in 1993. Since his mother's death when he was ten years old, Kyuquot has acted out against trainers several times.

Sakari. Born at SeaWorld San Antonio in 2010, Sakari has had problems with self-destructive behaviors.

Takara. Born at SeaWorld San Diego in 1991 before ending up at SeaWorld San Antonio in 2009, Takara was relocated several times. She was separated from her mother, Kasatka, and afterward, Kasatka sent out long-range vocals from her pool, presumably trying to communicate with Takara.

Tuar. Born at SeaWorld Orlando in 1999 and sent to SeaWorld San Antonio in 2004, Tuar has acted out against trainers and shown signs of boredom by picking at paint on the bottom of his pool.

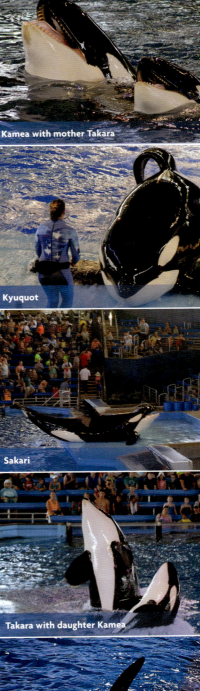

Kamea with mother Takara

Kyuquot

Sakari

Takara with daughter Kamea

Tuar

Amaya

Corky II

Ikaika

SEAWORLD SAN DIEGO

SeaWorld San Diego was founded in 1964 and has held orcas captive since 1965.

Amaya. Amaya was born at SeaWorld San Diego in 2014 during a rainstorm. Her name means "night rain" in Arabic.

Corky II. Born around 1966 and captured in 1969, Corky II was sent to Marineland of the Pacific in 1969 and was transferred to SeaWorld San Diego in 1987. She has been in captivity longer than any other orca.

Ikaika. Ikaika was born at SeaWorld Orlando in 2002 and sent to SeaWorld San Diego in 2011. Shortly after that, Ikaika was seen with a large gash on his chin, presumably from the metal barriers that trainers use.

Kalia. Kalia was born at SeaWorld San Diego in 2014. While pregnant at age ten, Kalia became stuck in one of the gates of her pen.

Keet. Keet was born at SeaWorld San Antonio in 1993 and sent to SeaWorld San Diego in 2012. Being the subdominant orca, Keet has been raked by other orcas in captivity with him. (Raking is when an orca's skin is scraped by the teeth of another orca during an aggressive attack to show dominance. It is very painful.)

Kalia

Keet (left)

Makani. Makani was born at SeaWorld San Diego in 2013. After her mother died when Makani was four years old, she could be seen with numerous rake marks from other orcas.

Nakai. Born at SeaWorld San Diego in 2001, Nakai lost a large chunk of flesh under his chin during a nighttime show, which was caused either by scraping a metal railing or engaging in an altercation with another orca.

Orkid. Born at SeaWorld San Diego in 1988, Orkid has pulled trainers to the bottom of her pool on several occasions. Losing her mother when she was only 11 months old could be the cause of her aggression.

Shouka. Born at Marineland Antibes (France) in 1993 and sent to SeaWorld San Diego in 2012, Shouka was the first orca born in captivity in Europe. She had no other orcas around her for the first ten years of her life.

Ulises. Born around 1977 and sent to SeaWorld San Diego in 1994, Ulises is the oldest male orca in captivity. He was alone for the first thirteen years of his life before he was sent to San Diego.

Makani

Nakai

Orkid

Shouka

Ulises

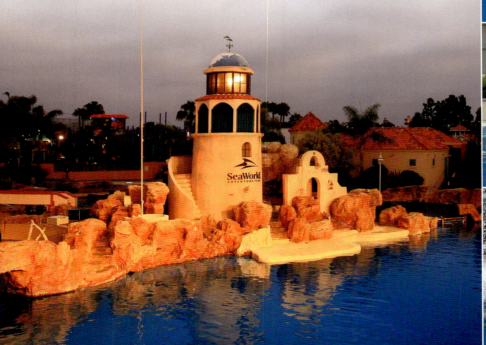

Inouk

Keijo

France

MARINELAND ANTIBES

Marineland Antibes, located on the French Riviera, was founded in 1970 but has held orcas captive since the year before that. In 2015, it was affected by a coastal flood in which a twenty-year-old orca perished.

Inouk. Born at Marineland Antibes in 1999, Inouk's dorsal fin has completely collapsed to the right side. After gnawing on the pool walls out of boredom for two decades, he has worn his teeth down to the pulp.

Keijo. Born at Marineland Antibes in 2013.

Moana. Born at Marineland Antibes in 2011.

Wikie. Wilkie was born at Marineland Antibes in 2001. In 2018, Wikie became the first orca recorded saying human phrases, such as *hello*, *bye-bye*, and *one, two, three*.

Moana

Wikie

Canada

MARINELAND

Marineland, located in Niagara Falls, Ontario, was founded in 1961 and has held orcas captive since 1972. In 2015, the Legislative Assembly of Ontario passed the Ontario Society for the Prevention of Cruelty to Animals Amendment Act, which prohibits the acquisition and breeding of orcas in Ontario.

Kiska. Born around 1976, Kiska was sent to Marineland in Ontario in 1979. She lives alone, as there are no other orcas at this park.

Kiska

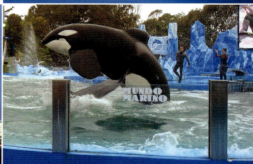

Argentina

MUNDO MARINO

Mundo Marino, located in Buenos Aires, was founded in 1978 and has held orcas captive since 1985.

Kshamenk. Born around 1988, Kshamenk was sent to Mundo Marino in 1992. Since 2000, he has had the company of only bottlenose dolphins and no other orcas.

Kshamenk

Adàn

Keto

Kohana

Ula and Morgan

Skyla

Tekoa

Spain

LORO PARQUE

Loro Parque, in the Canary Islands off the coast of northwest Africa, was founded in 1972 and has been holding orcas captive since 2006.

Adàn. Born in 2010, Adàn was the first orca to be born in captivity in Spain.

Keto. Born in 1995 and sent to Loro Parque in 2006, Keto was moved among all four SeaWorld parks and has had difficulty with aggression toward trainers.

Kohana. Born in 2002, Kohana was sent to Loro Parque in 2006.

Morgan. Born around 2007 and sent to Loro Parque in 2011, Morgan has had problems repeatedly ramming her gate.

Skyla. Born in 2004 and sent to Loro Parque in 2006, Skyla was separated from her mother when she was only two.

Tekoa. Born in 2000, Tekoa was sent to Loro Parque in 2006. Because of past aggression, no trainers are allowed in the water with him.

Ula. Born at Loro Parque in 2018, Ula was born with a skin discoloration problem and suffers from skin infections as a result.

Lara

Japan

KAMOGAWA SEA WORLD

Kamogawa Sea World is located near Tokyo. It was founded in 2000 and has been holding orcas captive since that time. It is the only park in the world that still allows trainers in the water with the orcas.

Lara. Lara was born at Kamogawa Sea World in 2001. Lara's mother was taken away from her when she was only ten months old.

Lovey. This female orca was born in 1998.

Luna. Born at Kamogawa Sea World in 2012, Luna is currently the youngest orca there.

Ran II. Ran II was born at Kamogawa Sea World in 2006. Both Lovey and Lara are her sisters.

PORT OF NAGOYA PUBLIC AQUARIUM

Located in southern Japan, the Port of Nagoya Public Aquarium was founded in 1992 and has held orcas captive since 2003.

Earth. Earth was born in Kamogawa Sea World in 2008 and sent to Port of Nagoya Public Aquarium in 2015. Because of his mother's aggressive behavior toward him, he had to be separated from her, and he eventually spent several years in isolation.

Rin/Lynn. Rin was born at Port of Nagoya Public Aquarium in 2012. A public vote changed her name to Lynn, but you can find both names in use.

Stella. Born near Iceland around 1986 and sent to Port of Nagoya Public Aquarium in 2011, Stella spent twenty-four years in Kamogawa Sea World before being moved to Nagoya.

Lovey

Luna

Lynn and Ran II

Earth

Rin/Lynn

Stella and pod

Naja

Narnia

Russia

MOSKVARIUM

Moskvarium in Moscow was founded in 1935 and has held orcas captive since 2013.

Naja. Naja was born around 2010 and sent to Moskvarium in 2014.

Narnia. Narnia was born around 2007 and sent to Moskvarium in 2014. There were plans to have her perform at the Sochi Olympics in 2014, but public outcry prevented this from happening.

Nord. Nord was born around 2008 and sent to Moskvarium in 2014.

SEASIDE DOLPHINARIUM

Located on the eastern coast of Russia, north of Korea and west of Japan, Seaside Dolphinarium was the site of an illegal capture of eleven orcas and eight-seven beluga whales. Public outcry prompted their release and fines were imposed on some of the companies involved.

Malvina. Malvina was born around 2012 and sent to Seaside Dolphinarium in 2015. At this time her location cannot be confirmed.

Nord

Malvina

China

There are seventy-eight marine mammal parks in China and another twenty-six are currently under construction.

CHIMELONG OCEAN KINGDOM

Chimelong Ocean Kingdom is located on the coast of mainland China, south of Hong Kong. It was founded in 2014 and is supposed to have nine orcas, but little is known about them.

Chimelong orca

SHANGHAI HAICHANG OCEAN PARK

Shanghai Haichang Ocean Park is located on the coast of mainland China, just south of the city of Shanghai. It was founded in 2018 and is holding two orcas (Dora and Wow) captive, along with two other unnamed orcas.

WUXI CHANGQIAO OCEAN KINGDOM

Wuxi Changqiao Ocean Kingdom is located inland, west of Shanghai, and was founded in 2019. It holds two unnamed orcas captive.

Shanghai orcas

Wuxi Orca

5

What We Can Do to Protect Orcas

Because orca trainers have been injured or killed by getting into orca tanks at marine parks and performing tricks in the water (known as waterworks) with the orcas, the US government decided to prohibit this activity. However, the parks have been using these stunts as a way to draw crowds and make money. Without these shows, parks are having to rethink whether it's feasible to continue holding orcas in captivity. But what else would they do with them?

Some people believe that the orcas should remain in captivity but just not perform during shows. Others have argued for the release of all captive orcas; however, this is nearly impossible. Most of the orcas have drilled teeth, making them prone to infection and, in some cases, incapable of catching fish.

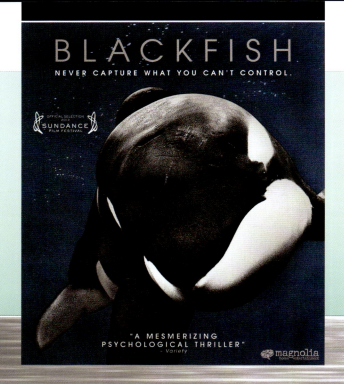

Blackfish is a documentary that has drastically changed the way much of the public views marine parks. (See the resources on page 39.) It gives viewers a look into the real life of captive orcas at parks such as SeaWorld. The movie goes back in time and details how Pacific Northwest orcas were abducted and separated from their families in the early 1970s. The focus of the movie is Tilikum's life of enslavement (see page 12), beginning with his mistreatment at Sealand of the Pacific and moving on to SeaWorld.

Reintroducing Orcas into the Ocean

W e at Sea Shepherd would like to propose a compromise. We believe that all the captive orcas deserve to live out the remainder of their lives in freedom, and a viable option would be sea pens. These pens could be created by netting off small coves, or bays, possibly in areas of the Pacific Northwest, where many captive orcas are originally from. The orcas would have the opportunity to learn how to catch fish, swim in ocean water, and dive to deep depths. SeaWorld trainers would still be on hand to assess their health and progress, and customers could still be charged to enter the park and see the orcas living a more natural lifestyle. If the sea pen rehabilitation process shows promise and the whereabouts of the captives' relatives are known, perhaps at some point certain orcas could be released back into open water.

Orca Watching

Whale watching began in the 1950s, when a fisherman took people out to see the gray whale migration. It has since turned into a more than $2 billion global industry with over thirteen million ecotourists enjoying the pastime each year. Watching both orcas and whales is a great alternative to going to an amusement park, and you can get a close-up look at orcas in their natural environment.

You can also see how true pods interact with each other; listen on hydrophones to hear them communicating; and watch them feed, play, and perform natural behaviors instead of learned tricks for food. It's a pleasure to watch them swim off into the sunset rather than to leave a park with a terrible feeling about the conditions there.

It's possible to watch orcas in some places without having to board a boat. There are islands between Seattle, Washington, and Victoria, British Columbia, where you can observe orcas swim right past the shore as they search for Chinook salmon between May and October. If you travel to nearby San Juan Island, you can also stop by The Whale Museum in the town of Friday Harbor, Washington, to learn about southern resident orcas and listen to guest speakers talk about their research in the Puget Sound.

On the following page is a list of the most common places around the world to see orcas, but these are by no means the only locations where you can find them. Orcas can be located anywhere in the ocean, so chances are good that you can find them in the waters closest to you!

UNITED STATES

Seward, Alaska
Dana Point, California
Long Beach, California
Marina del Ray, California
Monterey Bay, California
Newport Beach, California
Redondo Beach, California
Santa Barbara, California
Hawaiian Islands
Depoe Bay, Oregon
Newport, Oregon
Pacific City, Oregon
Anacortes, Washington
Bellingham, Washington
Everett, Washington
San Juan Island, Washington
Seattle, Washington

CANADA

British Columbia
Labrador
Newfoundland
Nova Scotia
Quebec

CARIBBEAN

Dominica

CENTRAL AND SOUTH AMERICA

Valdes Peninsula, Argentina
Brunswick Peninsula, Chile
Osa Peninsula, Costa Rica

AFRICA

Cape Town, South Africa

ORCA WATCHING AROUND THE WORLD

EUROPE

Húsavík, Iceland
Reykjavík, Iceland
West Cork, Ireland
Ofotfjord, Norway
Tysfjord, Norway
Vest Fjord, Norway
Algarve, Portugal
Azores, Portugal
Caithness, Scotland
Orkney, Scotland
Shetland Islands, Scotland

JAPAN

Chōshi
Sea of Japan

AUSTRALIA AND NEW ZEALAND

Bruny Island, Tasmania, Australia
Eden, New South Wales, Australia
Western Australia
Auckland, New Zealand
Kaikōura, New Zealand
Wellington, New Zealand

OTHER

Antarctica
Barents Sea
Bering Sea
Chukchi Sea
Greenland
Sea of Okhotsk

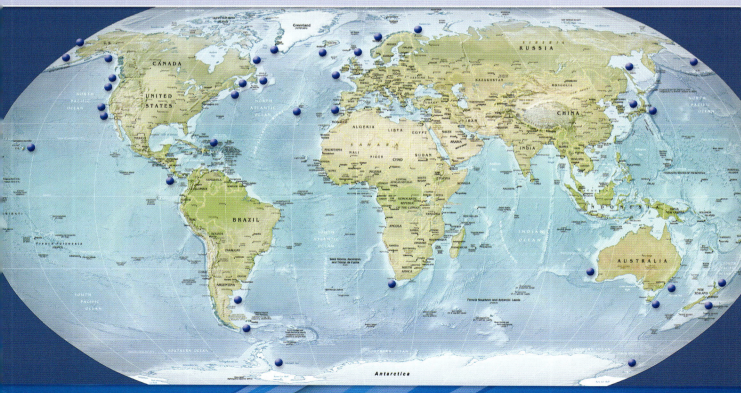

RESOURCES

CONSERVATION GROUPS

Sea Shepherd Conservation Society. Founded in 1977 by Captain Paul Watson to intervene and stop illegal activities that exploit marine wildlife.

seashepherd.org

Sea Shepherd France. Focused on closing Marineland in Antibes through education and litigation.

seashepherd.fr

Dolphin Project. Its mission is to end dolphin exploitation and slaughter.

dolphinproject.com

Earth Island Institute. The organization that freed Keiko from captivity.

earthisland.org

Oceanic Preservation Society. Creates films and inspires awareness through visual displays. Producer of the Academy Award–winning film *The Cove*.

opsociety.org

Orca Research Trust (New Zealand). Protects orcas and their habitats through conservation, education, and scientific research.

orcaresearch.org

Orcalab (Canada). Supports orca conservation and research without interfering with their lives or habitats.

orcalab.org

Whale Sanctuary Project. Develops marine sanctuaries for orcas in order to facilitate their release into the wild.

whalesanctuaryproject.org

PROTECTION ACTS

The Convention on International Trade in Endangered Species of Wild Flora and Fauna (CITES)

cites.org

The Marine Mammal Protection Act (MMPA) and the **Endangered Species Act (ESA)**

fisheries.noaa.gov/topic/laws-policies

Oceans Protection Plan (Canada)

tc.canada.ca/en/initiatives/oceans-protection-plan

INFORMATION ON ORCAS

Blackfish. Documentary on the real lives of orcas in captivity.

Live Science

livescience.com/27431-orcas-killer-whales.html

National Oceanic and Atmospheric Administration (NOAA)

fisheries.noaa.gov/species/killer-whale#overview

Whale and Dolphin Conservation

us.whales.org/whales-dolphins/species- guide/orca-killer-whale

ABOUT THE AUTHORS

Captain Paul Watson is a Canadian American marine conservation activist who founded the direct-action group Sea Shepherd Conservation Society in 1977. He has been described by Farley Mowat, author of *Never Cry Wolf*, as "the world's most aggressive, most determined, most active, and most effective defender of wildlife."

Tiffany Humphrey has been working with marine wildlife since 2003 in South Carolina, Washington State, and Hawaii. From 2009 to 2013, she worked as Paul's executive assistant at Sea Shepherd Conservation Society.

INDEX

Photo credits (left to right, top to bottom): *Page i,* 123RF; *page iv,* 123RF; *page 1,* 123RF, 123RF; *page 2,* 123RF, 123RF; *page 3,* 123RF, Shutterstock, 123RF; *page 4,* NOAA's Ocean Service, Alaska Resources Library & Information Services (ARLIS), ARLIS, 123RF; *page 5,* Sea Shepherd, Australian Customs and Border Protection, Sea Shepherd, Sea Shepherd, Sea Shepherd, Wikimedia Commons; *page 6,* Getty Images, Sea Shepherd, Sea Shepherd, Sea Shepherd, Sea Shepherd; *page 7,* 123RF, 123RF, 123RF, 123RF; *page 8,* 123RF; *page 9,* Far Eastern Russian Orca Project (FEROP), Wikimedia Commons; *page 10,* 123RF, Wallie Funk, Washington State Archives, Wallie Funk, 123RF; *page 11,* David Phillips, Terrell Newby, Hah; *page 12,* United Artists, 123RF, Wikimedia Commons, Lauren Bernhardt-Rhone; *page 13,* Wikimedia Commons, Sea Shepherd, Sea Shepherd, Sea Shepherd; *page 14,* 123RF; *page 15,* 123RF, FEROP; *page 16,* Sea Shepherd, 123RF, www.cestassez.fr, Sea Shepherd; *page 17,* marineland.fr, Britta Lenzner, 123RF, 123RF; *page 18,* 123RF, Ingrid Visser, Sea Shepherd, simplyloveorcas.com, Wikimedia Commons; *page 19,* 123RF, Ian Griffiths, 123RF, 123RF; *page 20,* 123RF; *page 21,* 123RF, Kimmy Vengeance; *page 22,* Heather Jordan, PETA, Olaf Schmidt, Tiffany Humphrey, Sea Shepherd, Tiffany Humphrey, Sea Shepherd, Britta Lenzner, Joel Rojas; *page 23,* Risha Fox, Anonymous, Anonymous, 123RF, Sea Shepherd, Ngchilkit, Wuxi, Anonymous, 123RF; *page 24,* Lauren Bernhardt-Rhone, 123RF, Samantha Cornwall, Samantha Cornwall, Samantha Cornwall, Samantha Cornwall, Averette; *page 25,* 123RF, PETA, PETA, PETA, PETA, Creative Commons, Sara Farrell; *page 26,* Anonymous, 123RF, Anonymous, Samantha Cornwall, Anonymous, PETA, 123RF; *page 27,* Anonymous, Samantha Cornwall, Sara Farrell, Heather Jordan, 123RF, Samantha Cornwall; *page 28,* Stefan Jacobs, 123RF, Hah, Sea Shepherd, Stefan Jacobs, Andreas Ahrens; *page 29,* 123RF, TinoPup, Jessica Shvimer, 123RF, Mundo Marino, Sea Shepherd; *page 30,* PETA, 123RF, Britta Lenzner, Britta Lenzner, Britta Lenzner, PETA, PETA, 123RF; *page 31,* 123RF, Hah, Hah, Hah, Hah, Hah, Hah, Hah; *page 32,* Risha Fox, 123RF, Risha Fox, Risha Fox, Unknown, Shutterstock; *page 33,* 123RF, 123RF, Chinese News, China Orca News, thecoasterkings.com, Wuxi; *page 34,* 123RF; *page 35,* 123RF, 123RF; *page 36,* Magnolia Pictures, 123RF; *page 37,* 123RF, 123RF; *page 38,* 123RF, 123RF; *page 40,* 123RF.

GROUNDSWELL BOOKS
SOLUTIONS FOR A SUSTAINABLE WORLD

For more books that inspire readers to create a healthy, sustainable planet for future generations,
visit BookPubCo.com.

**Our planet's environmental problems have reached the crisis level.
In response, we developed two vital series to help educate, empower, and motivate everyone to take action.**

PLANET IN CRISIS SERIES

Addresses urgent challenges of climate change by focusing on specific issues, identifying their impacts, and illustrating creative solutions that can make a difference.

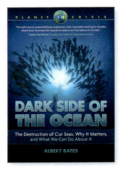

Dark Side of the Ocean
Albert Bates
978-1-57067-394-8 • $12.95

Transforming Plastic
Albert Bates
978-1-57067-371-9 • $9.95

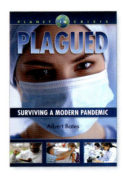

Plagued
Albert Bates
978-1-57067-400-6 • $9.95

PLANETARY SOLUTIONS SERIES

Inspires young people to understand, challenge, and solve the environmental problems that put the Earth at risk.

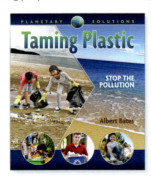

Taming Plastic
Albert Bates
978-1-939053-24-4 • $14.95

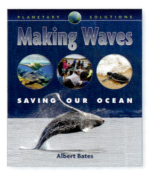

Making Waves
Albert Bates
978-1-939053-33-6 • $14.95

Purchase these titles from your favorite book source or buy them directly from:
Book Publishing Company • PO Box 99 • Summertown, TN 38483 • 1-888-260-8458
Free shipping and handling on all orders.